INSPIRING MOTIVATION FOR

Happiness, Health, & Wealth

An inspiring story along with quotes and resources to help achieve your dream life

TRINA I. WEEDEN

Copyright © 2017 Trina I. Weeden

ISBN: 978-0-578-76295-1

Written in 2017 by Trina I Weeden
Published and printed in United States in 2020
Publisher: Trina I Weeden
Email: Treewee1205@gmail.com
Designed and Formatted by Nonon Tech & Design

Printed in the United States of America

Table of Contents

About Me

HAVE BEEN married for 28 years to an amazing man. I have two adult children and a very handsome grandson. I have always been the kind of person to go after what I wanted in life; dreaming big and wanting it all. I wanted nothing but the best for family and friends, and ensured I made it known. I truly believe you can have whatever you want in life if you really have a desire for it. This is my story of how I found Happiness, Health and Wealth.

And you will too!

I would like to dedicate this book to my husband Ray Weeden, my children Michael and Tiyana Weeden and my grandson Daniel Weeden. I love you guys with all my heart. Always remember, you can do, be and have whatever it is you want, you just have to want it and believe you can have it.

I am a very passionate and creative person who enjoys organizing, planning and decorating. I love seeing smiles on people faces and I get emotional over happy moments and happy endings. I am very caring and giving (a trait I get from my Father) and can also be very sensitive at times which my husband often teases me for. I would cry during sitcom episodes we've watched a thousand times. Please don't show the wedding episode of **A Different World**, or the last episode of **Friends** when Rachel got off the plane. And who can forget the series finale of **Good Times** when the family were all finally leaving the "Ghetto" and Thelma announced she was pregnant, OMG the water works never stop. That's only a few of thousands that have me in tears over and over again. If the result is happiness, find me a tissue because the inevitable will happen.

It's not always tears with TV or movies; I get excited if I see an elegantly decorated room, or a real awesome looking vase. I look forward to watching some of my favorite episodes on HGTV or DIY. Sometimes, a perfect day is a day I'm out looking at model homes or shopping at Z Gallerie or Home Goods. If anyone mentions they are getting ready to redecorate or buy some new furniture, I get so excited for them, and want to be a part of their journey. I am very excited for people when they share good news with me. People's happiness makes me happy.

I have always been grateful for everything I have in life. Even when things didn't always go my way, I was still appreciative for what was there. It was very easy to find this journey of my life, because I was always heading this way. Instead of getting frustrated sitting in traffic, I would be grateful I can listen to my playlist a little longer.

I never let the ugly in others, ruin the beauty in me. I simply respond to rude people with a smile and a "enjoy your day".

Happiness, Heath and Wealth are all within your reach. You have to look inside yourself to find it.

Intro

> *"The Lotus rises on its stalk unsoiled by the mud and water, so the wise one speaks of peace and is unstained by the opinions of the world"*
>
> - BUDDHA

I CAN REMEMBER sitting at my desk at work not really doing anything at all, just searching the internet trying to plan my next big event or deciding on what room I wanted to decorate next. I realized the only time I was truly enjoying my job was when I was doing this or talking to a fellow co-worker about our passions.

Although my job was great (some people would say I had it made) I worked in the Payroll/HR department of a large hotel chain. I was close to home, my hours were 7:00am – 3:30pm, parking and lunch were free, and the perks were very nice. I still found myself wanting more, I wasn't fulfilled. There was nothing stressful about my job, it just wasn't my passion.

My coworkers constantly told me I was great at what I did and my patience and listening skills were amazing. There were many complaints and a few irate situations working in the department I was in, but never once did my calm demeanor waiver. My main goal was to ensure people left my office feeling ten times better or at least satisfied knowing their situation was going to be resolved. I always aimed to please and strived for satisfaction.

I would receive gifts and items of appreciation from co workers all the time and this confirmed I was doing an excellent job.

During the times when it was quiet, I would sit for several minutes with my office door closed enjoying the relaxation and peacefulness. This was so amazing and led me to do more research on the world of meditating. This is where I learned about positive energy, vibrations and visualizations. There were several movies, audios, quotes and books on these subjects, but the one thing that stuck out the most was a quote about paying attention to your vibrations around people and situations. I noticed the people whom I had to work closely with every day were bringing a dark feeling to my vibrations and energy. It's true what they say "Misery Loves Company", but I refused to take a seat on that couch.

I am such a happy person by nature, and never would allow someone's behavior or negative attitude take me out of character.

Things really start to change when I was witnessing actions and behaviors that were, in my opinion "integrity questionable", that's when I knew it was time to move on. Don't get me wrong, there were a few people I chose to spend a little more time with, their energy was positive, and I would always receive good vibes when in their presence. I would share quotes and provide them with positive words of encouragement whenever they asked or seemed to need it. They seemed very receptive and this made me happy.

Like millions of others, I had everyday financial obligations, mortgage, college tuition, medical bills etc., so I knew I needed a source of income. I was very clear on what I was passionate about and what I wanted to do. I just needed to take that step. I would create vision boards on the things I wanted to have and achieve and keep them where I can view them regularly. I kept one in my office, one in my bedroom, one in the family room and one in my closet. I have a total of 4 vision boards to date. I wanted to be sure they were seen by me daily and I would schedule a time every day to look at my vision boards and visualize on my goals and the things I wanted to achieve.

Visualizing was so exciting for me, I have been doing it all my life (we all have) but never realized it.

Visualizing is like mentally shopping for the things you want. Think of the things you want and imagine having them. If you are passionate about it, the feelings are gratifying. There is a little more to it, but that's the basics. So, visualize away.

I kept a journal which played a major role in my life also. I would write every day about the things I was grateful for as well as the goals I wanted to achieve. I started keeping a journal in 2012; I have a total of 16 journals to date and not a day goes by that I don't write in my journal. My routine was; once I was completely ready for bed, I would plug in my ear phones tune in to some sort of relaxation sounds (I choose to listen to Baroque classical music or ocean waves) and write in my journal. This proved to be very exciting and satisfying. If I ever missed a day, I would just double up the next day, but believe me I hardly ever missed one. I would give journals out as gifts, especially to some of the younger people in my life. I would express to them to share their feelings by writing them down in a journal instead of on social media. We all have things we need to get off our chest, but sometimes you can't share with everyone. Writing in a journal is very therapeutic and relaxing. So, grab a journal and write until your hearts content.

Meditation is also a regular for me. I would take time out to meditate at least 3 to 4 times a week for at least 10 to 15 minutes each time. Meditation is not an easy process and it may take a while to do it correctly, but once you learn how, it's so amazing. I developed my own routine of meditating and relaxing. I would always be sure to wait until I knew I would not be disturbed and usually go into the guest room, light a candle and begin my session. Sometimes I would be so relaxed, it would last for 30 minutes or so. The bath tub was another area I would meditate; those were the longer sessions. Once you sink down in the hot steaming water, your body relaxes and you can get lost in your own world, I know I did.

I would always end each session with a set of positive affirmations. Now meditation may not be for everyone, it definitely takes patience and discipline, but for those who discover it: it can be life changing.

Meditation helps you to notice signs you may not have before. You know the saying if you sit still long enough the answer or solution will come. Well believe me it's true.

One day while watching one of my favorite inspirational movies, which by the way I've watched several times, it happened; I heard the quote that would change my life. The quote simply stated,

"Take the first step in faith. You don't have to see the whole staircase, just take the first step"

– DR. MARTIN LUTHER KING JR.

I still get chill bumps when I read or hear this. I decided to submit my letter of resignation, packed up my vision board and live the life I love.

I have so many people to thank for supporting, encouraging and believing in me throughout this whole journey. First, my husband Ray, words can not begin to express how grateful I am to him. He allowed me to follow my dreams and stood by me every step of the way. His workload became bigger and heavier but not once did he complain. He is and will always be my rock. Bless his Heart (inside joke) smiles!!!!

I also have to thank my love circle; Roseta Lee, Melissa Dawson, Crystal Williams, Yolanda Randolph, Colette Hawley, Shannen Weeden, Tamiko McCants, Crystal Shepherd and Alonzo Randolph. Oh My Goodness, these guys have been so supportive and motivating, each in their own and personalizing ways. They would say, you are great at planning, organizing and decorating and you always plan awesome events; you should start your own business. I was always very passionate about planning parties, events and gatherings. My children's birthday parties, family cookouts and dinner parties were all so amazing. I planned my own wedding in 1992 and my 15th wedding anniversary celebration in 2007.

So needless to say, I owned this special gift. These guys allowed me to plan major events for them or simply referred my services. They would assist me with events not knowing when or if they were getting compensated. They continuously encouraged me by listening to me repeatedly about my new ideas and what I wanted to achieve. They would always say "If anyone can, you can". Although their support and encouragement came in different shapes and forms, it motivated me to keep moving forward. I love them all and I will always be grateful for them.

Everyone has a passion for something, some people just can't or don't know how to spot it, or they simply just don't know what to do with it. If you surround yourself with the right people or situations, it will be made known. Sit still, meditate and the answer will surely come.

It's amazing how you see things much clearer when you change your environment and the people you surround yourself with.

I wasted too many years with people I thought were friends, only to discover the truth, but you live, and you learn. Mandy Hale said it best ***"You don't lose friends, because real friends can never be lost. You lose people masquerading as friends, and you're better for it"***. I am still grateful for these people, because in every situation there is a lesson to be learned. So, I thank them for the lesson; I'm much better for it.

My advice to anyone trying to start a new chapter in their life; spend time with positive people; people who are on the same journey as you or at least support the journey you're on. Find what motivates you the most and focus on it. Realize your dream life is a creation and not a competition. Never mind what someone else has or is doing; create your own happiness. The world is full of opportunity and abundance; it's all around us, just reach out and grab it.

You have within you to create your own life; you decide what it is you want most and go get it. This is true for Happiness, Health and Wealth. You have the power to heal yourself if you truly believe it. You can dwell on the illness and the illness will be there or you can focus on healing. Let the doctors and professionals deal with the illness.

Have you ever noticed when you are not feeling well, you lie in bed all day complaining about the symptoms and they seem to get worse? Try getting up, getting dress and acting as if you feel great, even if you don't. Trust me, this is very powerful. I first discovered this after watching one of my favorite movies that I will mention in a later chapter.

So, as the saying goes, you are what you think; so think Happiness, Health and Wealth. If you repeat something enough you will start to believe it, and once you believe it; it becomes reality. Repetition is key.

Today I am doing only what I love, living my dream life and blessing those around me. I have always dreamed of designing my own home and I am very happy to say we will be presenting it to an architect/custom builder soon. We have officially decided to name our new home **The W Manor**.

It's amazing what you can achieve if you really have the burning desire to do so, just remember to keep your energy and vibrations high. "Everything is Energy, your thought begins it, your emotion amplifies it, and your action increases the momentum.

"Match the frequency of the reality you want, and you cannot help but get that reality. It can be no other way. This is not philosophy, this is physics."

Your vibration is a way of describing your overall state of being. High vibrations happen when you have feelings of joy, gratitude, love etc. Low vibrations are feelings of anger, jealousy, sadness, fear.

I suggest you only visualize when your vibration is high, and remember meditating can help raise your vibration. Always put your heart mind and soul in all you do. Success is a journey, not a destination. Enjoy the journey!

Chapter One

Abundance

- » Extremely plentiful
- » Overflowing
- » Fulfilled

ABUNDANCE
· ·

"The closer you are to alignment of what you want the calmer it feels"

- ABRAHAM HICKS

"Talk as if what you want is in the process of coming"

- ABRAHAM HICKS

"When you arise in the morning, think of what a precious privilege it is to be alive – to breathe, to think, to enjoy, to love"

- MARKUS AURELIUS

ABUNDANCE
· ·

"True abundance isn't based on our net worth;
it's based on our self-worth"

- GABRIELLE BENSTEIN

"See yourself living in abundance and you will
attract it. It always works, every time with
every person"

- BOB PROCTOR

"Doing what you love is the cornerstone
of having abundance in your life"

- DR. WAYNE DYER

ABUNDANCE
....

"Like the air you breathe, abundance in all things is available to you. Your life will simply be as good as you allow it to be"

– ABRAHAM HICKS

"You are what you think. So think big, believe big, act big, give big, forgive big, love big and live big"

– ANDREW CARNEGIE

ABUNDANCE
· ·

"When you focus on being a blessing,
you are always blessed with abundance"

– JOEL OSTEEN

"Abundance is a state, not a quantity.
Idea of shortage is man made"

– AVTARJEET SINGH DHANJAL

"Abundance is not something we acquire.
It is something we tune into"

– DR. WAYNE DYER

ABUNDANCE

· ·

"You can become instantly successful with a simple thought, but long-lasting and pronounced success comes to those who renew their commitment to a mindset of abundance every minute of every hour of every day"

- BRYANT MCGILL

"Love what you do and do what you love. Passion is the key that opens the door to joy and abundance"

- DAVID CUSCHERIE

ABUNDANCE

"No more effort is required to aim high in life, to demand abundance and prosperity, than is required to accept misery and poverty"

- NAPOLEON HILL

"You must find a place within yourself where nothing is impossible: That's abundance"

- DEEPAK CHOPRA

ABUNDANCE

··

"The essence of this law is that you must think abundance, see abundance, feel abundance and believe abundance"

- ROBERT COLLIER

"Expect every need to be met, expect the answer to every problem, and expect abundance on every level"

- EILEEN CADDY

ABUNDANCE

·····························

"Self care is not selfish. We can not nurture others from a dry well. We need to take care of our own needs first, then we can give from our surplus, our abundance"

-JENNIFER LOUDEN

"Taking time to do nothing often brings everything into perspective"

- DOE ZANTAMATA

Chapter Two

Dreams

- » Imagination
- » Visions
- » Thoughts

DREAMS

· ·

"The biggest adventure you can take is to live the life of your dreams"

– OPRAH WINFREY

"The future belongs to those who believes in the beauty of their dreams"

– ELEANOR ROOSEVELT

"Every great dream begins with a dreamer. Always remember, you have within you the strength, the patience and the passion to reach for the stars and to change the world"

– HARRIET S. TUBMAN

DREAMS

· ·

"Ordinary people believe in the possible.
Extraordinary people imagine what others think
is impossible, and by imagining the impossible,
they begin to see it as possible"

- CHERRIE CARTER-SCOTT

"Whatever your dream is, every extra penny you
have needs to be going towards that"

- WILL SMITH

DREAMS
· ·

"Never mind what-is, imagine it the way you want it to be so that your vibration is a match to your desire"

\- ABRAHAM HICKS

"The ones crazy enough to think they can change the world, are the ones who do"

\- STEVE JOBS

"When your desires are strong enough, you will possess superhuman powers to achieve them"

\- NAPOLEON HILL

DREAMS

· ·

"If you don't build your dream, someone else will hire you to help them build theirs"

- DHIRUBHAI AMBANI

"Never let go of your dreams. Believe in your dreams, they were given to you for a reason"

- KATRINA MAYER

DREAMS
· ·

*"Start where you are. Use what you have.
Do what you can"*

- ARTHUR ASHE

*"Never limit yourself because of others limited
imagination; never limit others because of your
own limited imagination"*

- MAE JEMISON

*"You are never too old to set another goal or
dream a new dream"*

- C.S. LEWIS

DREAMS

....

"All your dreams can come true, if you have the courage to pursue them"

- WALT DISNEY

"A dream becomes a goal when action is taken towards its achievement"

- BO BENNETT

"Dreams and dedication are a powerful combination"

- WILLIAM LONGGOOD

Chapter Three

Faith

- » Loyalty
- » Belief
- » Assurance

FAITH
....

"Every mountain top is within reach if you just keep climbing"

- BARRY FINLAY

"You don't have to be great to start, but you have to start to be great"

- ZIG ZAGLER

"Sometimes the smallest step in the right direction ends up being the biggest step of your life. Tip toe if you must, but take the step"

- ANDREA REISER

FAITH

· ·

"When you reach the end of your rope,
tie a knot and hang on"

‑ THOMAS JEFFERSON

"If you are persistent, you will get it.
If you are consistent you will keep it"

‑ HARVEY MCKAY

"Always go with your passions.
Never ask yourself if it's realistic or not"

‑ DEEPAK CHOPRA

FAITH

· ·

"Worry looks around. Regret looks back.
Faith looks forward"

- KREXY

"Optimism is the faith that leads to achievement.
Nothing can be done without hope and
confidence"

- HELEN KELLER

"Sometimes your only available transportation is
a leap of faith"

- MARGARET SHEPARD

FAITH

· ·

"If you can't fly then run. If you can't run then walk. If you can't walk then crawl, bur whatever you do you have to keep moving forward"

- DR. MARTIN LUTHER KING JR.

"Never stop trying. Never stop believing. Never give up. Your day will come"

- MANDY HALE

FAITH
· ·

"By believing passionately in something, we create it. The nonexistent is what we have not sufficiently desired"

- FRANZ KAFKA

"Logic will get you from A to B. Imagination will take you everywhere"

- ALBERT EINSTEIN

"Faith is the art of holding onto things in spite of your changing mood and circumstances"

- C.S. LEWIS

FAITH

· ·

"Faith is seeing the light when all your eyes see is darkness"

- UNKNOWN

"Faith is to believe what you do not see; the reward of this is to see what you believe"

- SAINT AUGUSTINE

"Hope is wishing something will happen. Faith believing something will happen. Courage is making something happen"

- UNKNOWN

FAITH
· ·

"The most profitable way to invest in your future is to have faith"

- STORMIE OMARITAN

"Belief and Faith opens doors to opportunities that were completely invisible without them"

- DOE ZANTAMATA

"Faith sees the invisible, believes the unbelievable and receives the impossible"

- CORRIE TEN BOOM

Chapter Four

Gratitude

- » Praise
- » Thankfulness
- » Honor

GRATITUDE
· ·

"Gratitude in advance is the most powerful creative force in the universe"

- NEIL DONALD WALSH

"Gratitude is the most medicinal emotions we can feel. It elevates our moods and fills us with joy"

- SARA AVANT STOVER

"All we have is all we need. All we need is the awareness of how blessed we really are"

- SARAH BAN BREATHNACH

GRATITUDE
· ·

"Gratitude is the single most important ingredient for living a successful and fulfilled life"

- JACK CANFIELD

"Gratitude can transform common days into thanksgivings, turn routine jobs into joy and change ordinary opportunities into blessings"

- WM ARTHUR WARD

GRATITUDE
· ·

"The vibration of gratitude attracts more positive things in your life"

\- CHERIE ROE DIRKSEN

"Your ability to see beauty and possibility is proportionate to the level in which you embrace gratitude"

\- DR. STEVE MARABOLI

"Change your expectation to appreciation and the world changes instantly"

\- TONY ROBBINS

GRATITUDE

· ·

"If you put gratitude at the center of your life.
One day you'll find it has completely taken over
your life"

- UNKNOWN

"Gratitude is one of the sweet shortcuts to
finding peace of mind and happiness inside.
No matter what is going on outside of us, there is
always something we can be grateful for"

- BARRY NEIL KAUFMAN

GRATITUDE
· ·

"I would maintain that Thanks are the highest form of thought; and that Gratitude is happiness doubled by wonder"

- G.K. CHESTERTON

"Gratitude is the healthiest of all human emotions. The more you express gratitude for what you have; you will have more to express gratitude for"

- ZIG ZAGLER

GRATITUDE

· ·

"Gratitude makes sense of our past, brings peace to today, and creates a vision for tomorrow"

- MELODY BEATTIE

"Learn to be grateful for what you have while pursuing what you want"

- JIM ROHN

"Talking about our problem is our greatest addiction. Break the habit, talk about your joys"

- RITA SCHIANO

GRATITUDE

· ·

*"Gratitude opens the door to the power,
the wisdom, the creativity, of the universe.
You open the door through gratitude"*

- DEEPAK CHOPRA

*"There are two ways to live your life.
One is as though nothing is a miracle.
The other is though everything is a miracle"*

- ALBERT EINSTEIN

GRATITUDE

· ·

"Enjoy the little things, for one day you will look back and realize they were the big things"

- ROBERT BRAULT

"Develop an attitude of gratitude, and give thanks for everything, knowing that every step is a step towards bigger and better things"

- BRIAN TRACEY

Chapter Five

Happiness

- » Bliss
- » Peace of Mind
- » Joy

HAPPINESS

· ·

"Very little is needed to make a happy life, it is all within yourself, in your way of thinking"

- MARKUS AURELIUS

"Choose a job you love, and you'll never have to work a day in your life"

- CONFUCIUS

"The most valuable skill or talent that you could develop is that of directing your thoughts towards what you want"

- ABRAHAM HICKS

HAPPINESS

· ·

"How to be happy; Decide every morning that you're in a good mood"

- UNKNOWN

"Find something that's makes you happy and think about it a lot"

- ABRAHAM HICKS

"Only the pursuit of Happiness is guaranteed, the rest is up to you"

- DAVID T FAGAN

HAPPINESS

· ·

"Happiness is an inside job. Don't assign anyone else that much power"

- MANDY HALE

"Happiness is the secret to all beauty. There is no beauty without happiness"

- CHRISTIAN DIOR

"Decide what you want. Believe you can have it. Believe you deserve it and believe it's possible for you"

- JACK CANFIELD

HAPPINESS

· ·

"Happiness is like a butterfly…when you go after it, it flies away…
But when you stand still….It comes to you.
A still mind is a happy mind"

– RASHIKA JAIN

"Happiness does not rely on what you have or who you are. It solely relies on what you think"

– BUDDHA

HAPPINESS
· ·

"If you want to live a happy life, tie it to a goal, not to people or objects"

- ALBERT EINSTEIN

"To enjoy good health, to bring true happiness to one's family, to bring peace to all, one must first discipline and control the mind.
If you can control your mind, you will find the way to enlightenment, and all wisdom and virtue will come to you"

- BUDDHA

HAPPINESS

· ·

"Choose your thoughts carefully. Keep what brings you peace, release what brings suffering and know that happiness is just a thought away"

- NISHAN PANWAR

"The key to being happy is knowing you have the power to choose what to accept and what to let go"

- DODINSKY

"Happiness held is the seed. Happiness shared is the flower"

- JOHN HARRIGAN

Chapter Six

Love

- » Fondness
- » Affection
- » Adoration

LOVE

· ·

*"Beauty begins the moment
you decide to be yourself"*

- CoCo Chanel

*"Life is not measure by the breaths we take but
by the moments that take our breath away"*

- Maya Angelou

"Love the life you live. Live the life you love"

- Bob Marley

LOVE

· ·

"People will forget what you said. People will forget what you did. But people will never forget how you made them feel"

\- MAYA ANGELOU

"Give, but don't allow yourself to be used. Love, but don't allow your heart to be abused. Trust, but don't be naïve. Listen, but don't lose you voice"

\- UNKNOWN

LOVE
· ·

"Attract what you expect. Reflect what you desire. Become what you respect. Mirror what you admire"

– UNKNOWN

"The most beautiful things in life can not be seen or touched; they must be felt with the heart"

– HELEN KELLER

"Love and compassion are necessities not luxuries. Without them humanity can not survive"

– DALAI LUMA

LOVE

·······························

"Let yourself be silently drawn by the strange
pull of what you love. It will not lead you astray"

– RUMI

"Learn to love without condition. Talk without
bad intention. Give without any reason.
Love without expectation"

– UNKNOWN

"If you want to know where your heart is,
look where you mind goes when it wanders"

– BERNARD BYER

LOVE

· ·

"Love is the condition in which the happiness of another person is essential to your own"

- ROBERT A. HEINLEIN

"Use your voice for kindness, your ears for compassion, your hands for charity and your heart for love"

- UNKNOWN

"The greatest gift you can give to others is the gift of unconditional love and acceptance"

- BRIAN TRACY

LOVE

· ·

"Change is sometimes needed to better yourself,
love yourself and truly be happy.
Never stop working on the best you can be.
It's a life long endeavor"

- ANGELIQUE LAFOREST TREMBLAY

"Our love is sharpened by the stone of our
challenges and strengthened by the struggles of
our growth"

- STEVE MARABOLT

Chapter Seven

Motivation

- » Encouragement
- » Interest
- » Drive

MOTIVATION
· ·

*"When you need something to believe in,
start with yourself"*

- ZACH AARONSON

*"Motivation is what gets you started.
Habit is what keeps you going"*

- JIM ROHN

*"When everything seems like an uphill struggle.
Just think of the view from the top"*

- UNKNOWN

MOTIVATION

....

"A goal should scare you a little and excite you a lot"

- JOE VITALE

"Be addicted to constant and never-ending self improvement"

- ANTHONY J D'ANGELO

"Just believe in yourself. Even if you don't, just pretend that you do and at some point you will"

- VENUS WILLIAMS

MOTIVATION
· ·

"When you want to succeed as bad as you want to breathe, then you'll be successful"

- ERIC THOMAS

"Do what you have to do until you can do what you need to do"

- OPRAH WINFREY

"The starting point of all achievement is desire"

- NAPOLEON HILL

MOTIVATION

· ·

"Get started, because a year from now you will wish you had started a year ago"

– KAREN LAMB

"Think big and don't listen to people who tell you it can't be done. Life is too short to think small"

– TIM FERRISS

"When you feel like quitting think about why you started"

– UNKNOWN

MOTIVATION
· ·

"Everything you need to be great is already inside you. Stop waiting for someone or something to light your fire. You have the match"

- DARREN HARDY

"Change will not come if you wait on some other person or some other time. You are the change you seek"

- BARACK OBAMA

Inspiring Motivation for Happiness Health & Wealth

MOTIVATION
· ·

"Stop being afraid of what could go wrong and start being excited about what could go right"

— TONY ROBBINS

"Every Pro was once an amateur.
Every Expert was once a beginner.
So dream big and start now"

— UNKNOWN

Chapter Eight

Patience

- » Persistent
- » Poise
- » Calmness

PATIENCE

· ·

"Patience is not the ability to wait, but the ability to keep a good attitude while you wait"

- JOYCE MEYER

"One who is a master of patience is a master of everything else"

- GEORGE SAVILE

"Patience, persistent and perspiration make an unbeatable combination for success"

- NAPOLEON HILL

PATIENCE

· ·

*"It might take a year, it might take a day,
but what's meant to be will always find a way"*

– KUSHANDWI ZDOM

*"Never make permanent decisions
on temporary feelings"*

– WIZ KHALIFA

"Adopt the pace of nature: its secret is patience"

– RALPH WALDO EMERSON

PATIENCE

· ·

"Patience is the calm acceptance that things can happen in a different order than the one you have in mind"

\- DAVID G. ALLEN

"A moment of patience in a moment of anger prevents a thousand moments of regret"

\- ALI IBN TALIB

PATIENCE
· ·

"The secret code of success is patience, a virtue that can not be replaced. It takes time to build great dreams"

- BERNARD KELVIN CLINE

"Inner peace is impossible without patience. Spiritual growth implies the mastery of patience. Patience allows the unfolding of destiny to proceed at its own unhurried pace"

- BRIAN WEISS

PATIENCE

· ·

"No road is too long for those who advances slowly and does not hurry, and no attainment is beyond his reach who equips patience to achieve it"

- JEAN DE LA BRUYERE

"Patience is a form of wisdom. It demonstrates that we understand and accept the fact that things unfold in their own time"

- JON KABAT ZINN

Chapter Nine

Positivity

- » Confidence
- » Eagerness
- » Absoluteness

POSITIVITY
· ·

"A great attitude becomes a great day which becomes a great month which becomes a great year which becomes a great life"

- MANDY HALE

"You must learn to master a new way to think before you can master a new way to be"

- MARIANNE WILLIAMSON

POSITIVITY

· ·

"The goal is to build up the wall of positivity so high around you that no matter what negativity comes your way it can't get through but bounces off and no longer affects your well being"

– SHARON RENE HUTCHINSON

"Find the good. It's all around you. Find it, showcase it and you'll start believing in it"

– JESSE OWENS

POSITIVITY

· ·

"The greatest weapon against stress is our ability to choose one thought over another"

\- WILLIAM JAMES

"Optimism is a happiness magnet. If you stay positive, good things and good people will be drawn to you"

\- MARY LOU RERRON

POSITIVITY

. . . .

"Keep your face to the sunshine and you can not see the shadow."

- HELEN KELLER

"Even the darkest night will end and the sun will rise"

- VICTOR HUGO

Always end every night with a positive attitude. No matter how hard things were, tomorrow's a fresh opportunity to make it better"

- UNKNOWN

POSITIVITY

· ·

"Choosing to be positive and having a great attitude is going to determine how you're going to live your life"

- JOEL OSTEEN

"You can have anything you want if you give up the belief that you can't"

- ROBERT ANTHONY

"Nurture your mind with great thoughts. For you will never go any higher than you think"

- BENJAMIN DISRAELI

POSITIVITY

....

"Keep your thoughts positive because your thoughts become your words. Keep your words positive because your words become your behavior. Keep your behavior positive because your behavior becomes your habits. Keep you habits positive because your habits become your values. Keep your values positive because your values become your destiny"

– MAHATMA GANDHI

Chapter Ten

Prosperity

- » Victory
- » Fortune
- » Blessings

PROSPERITY

· ·

"All prosperity begins in the mind and is dependent only upon the use of our creative imagination"

- RUTH ROSS

"Positive thinking and positive attitude attracts prosperity, peace and happiness. It exposes us towards achievements and success"

- ANURAG PRAKASH RAY

PROSPERITY
· ·

"It is because of our tranquil thoughts that we go to prosperity"

- GAUTAMA BUDDHA

"Prosperity is a mindset. It is your expectation. Expect to expand your wealth.....wealth of knowledge, relationships, income, and wisdom!"

- UNKNOWN

"One who acquires knowledge and passes it on to others, achieves success, happiness and prosperity"

- ATHARVA VEDA

PROSPERITY

· ·

"If there's a will, prosperity is not far behind"

- W. C. Fields

*"The only limits in life are those
we impose on ourselves"*

- Bob Proctor

*"If you're not excited about it,
it's not the right path"*

- Abraham Hicks

PROSPERITY

· ·

"Any person who contributes to prosperity must prosper in turn themselves"

\- EARL NIGHTINGALE

"Invent your world. Surround yourself with people, color, sounds and work that nourish you"

\- SARK

"Ask for what you want and be prepared to get it"

\- MAYA ANGELOU

PROSPERITY

· ·

"Prosperity is a way of living and thinking not just money and things. Poverty is a way of living and thinking, and not just lack of money and things"

- ERIC BUTTERWORTH

"The strongest single factor in prosperity consciousness is self-esteem; believing you can do it, believing you deserve it, believing you will get it"

- JERRY GILLIES

PROSPERITY

· ·

"Prosperity in the form of wealth works exactly the same as everything else.
You will see it coming into your life when you are unattached to needing it"

- WAYNE DYER

"Whatever we plant in our subconscious mind and nourish with repetition and emotion will one day become a reality"

- EARL NIGHTINGALE

PROSPERITY
· ·

"When you become passionately consumed with the vision that everything you do will prosper, it will in due time"

- CURTIS TYRONE JONES

"The things that excite you are not random. They are connected to your purpose. Follow them"

- UNKNOWN

Chapter Eleven

Vision

- » Perception
- » Sight
- » Image

VISION

· ·

*"Vision without action is merely a dream.
Action without vision just passes the time.
Vision with action can change the world"*

- JOEL A BARKER

*"Your vision will become clear only when you
look inside your heart.
He who looks inside awakens"*

- CARL JUNG

*"Never limit your vision based on
your current resources"*

- MICHAEL HYATT

VISION

· ·

"Create the highest grandest vision for your life; because you become what you believe"

– OPRAH WINFREY

"The tragedy of life doesn't lie on not reaching your goal. The tragedy lies in having no goal to reach"

– BENJAMIN MAYS

"Stop expecting your job to fund your vision. Your vision is probably bigger than your paycheck"

– T.D. JAKES

VISION
· ·

"Create a vision that makes you want to jump out of bed in the morning"

- UNKNOWN

"A great leader's courage to fulfill his vision comes from passion not position"

- JOHN MAXWELL

"Chase the vision not the money, the money will end up following you"

- TONY HSIEH

VISION

....

"When you visualize, you materialize.
If you've been there in the mind, you'll go there in
the body"

– DENIS WAITLEY

"Create in your mind a vision of what you want
and never take your eyes from it,
and the universe will cooperate with it"

– ABRAHAM HICKS

VISION

....

"You are more productive by doing 15 minutes of visualization, than from 16 hours of hard labor"

- ABRAHAM HICKS

"If you are working on something exciting that you really care about, you don't have to be pushed. The vision pulls you"

- STEVE JOBS

VISION

· ·

"Vision is the source of hope and life. The greatest gift ever given to mankind is not the gift of sight but the gift of vision. Sight is a function of the eyes; vision is a function of the heart. Eyes that look are common, but eyes that see are rare. Nothing noble or noteworthy on earth was ever done without vision"

- MYLES MUNROE

VISION

. . . .

"A vision is not just a picture of what could be;
it is an appeal to our better selves, a call to
become something more"

- ROSABETH MOSS KANTER

"A job is how you make money.
A career is how you make your mark.
A calling is how you acknowledge a higher
vision, whatever it may be"

- DEEPAK CHOPRA

VISION
· ·

"The power of imagination created the illusion that my vision went much further than the naked eye could see"

- NELSON MANDELA

"It's not what you look at that matters, it's what you see"

- HENRY DAVID THOREAU

VISION

·····························

"To bring anything into your life, imagine that it's already there"

- RICHARD BACH

"Be brave enough to live the life of your dreams according to your vision and purpose instead of the expectations and opinions of others"

- ROY BENNETT

Chapter Twelve

Wealth

- » Good Health
- » Good Fortune
- » Substantiality

WEALTH
··························

"True wealth is being able to do what I want when I want"

- JD ROTH

"If you are not willing to learn, no one can help you. If you are determined to learn, no one can stop you"

- ZIG ZIGLAR

"Wealth is the product of one's capacity to think"

- AYN RAND

WEALTH

······························

"Formal education will make you a living. Self education will make you a fortune"

- JOHN ROHN

"If you want to be rich…don't allow yourself the luxury of excuses"

- ROBERT KIYOSAKI

"Luxury must be comfortable. Otherwise it is not Luxury"

- COCO CHANEL

WEALTH

· ·

"People who have drawn wealth into their lives used The Secret, whether consciously or unconsciously. They think thoughts of abundance and wealth, and they do not allow contradictory thoughts to take root in their minds"

\- RHONDA BYNE

"My goal is to build a life I don't need a vacation from"

\- ROB HILL SR.

WEALTH

·····························

"Wealth is the ability to fully experience Life"

- HENRY DAVID THOREAU

"Those who work the whole day, have no time to make money"

- JOHN D. ROCKEFELLER

"The best things in life are free.
The second-best things are very expensive"

- COCO CHANEL

WEALTH

· ·

"It is better to start investing earlier in small increments rather than invest big increments at a later time"

- AYA LARAYA

"The first step in achieving Prosperity and Wealth is appreciating what you already have"

- SAMUEL RICHARDSON

"A wealthy person is simply a person who has learned to make money when they are not working"

- ROBERT KIYOSAKI

WEALTH

· ·

*"Thought is the only power which
can produce wealth"*

- WALLACE D. WATTLES

*"Invest in as much of yourself as you can,
you are your own biggest asset by far"*

- WARREN BUFFETT

*"There are three things you must do in order
to become wealthy. You must have the right
mindset, discover your purpose in life, and find a
business that expresses that purpose"*

- ANDY FUEHL

Chapter Thirteen

Resources

- » Movies
- » Books
- » Audios

Resources

"Learn to get in touch with the silence within yourself and know that everything in life has purpose. There are no mistakes, and no coincidences, all events are blessings given to us to learn from"

I have pulled motivation and inspiration from several different resources; books, movies, quotes and audios. It was these resources that encouraged me to start my own business and pursue the life of my dreams. It was not an easy process but definitely one worth going through.

I used the lotus flower throughout this book because of the meaning behind the symbol.

The Lotus Flower - Symbolizes beauty, fertility, prosperity, spirituality, and eternity. It's a sign of rebirth, and purity. The breaking of the surface every morning also suggests desire.

Here is a small list of resources which inspired and motivated me to keep moving forward. Please check out some of these and the many more available. They will change your life; they changed mine.

Movies

- » The Pursuit of Happyness - **2006**
- » Jobs – **2013**
- » The Secret - **2006**
- » The Opus - **2008**
- » I Am – **2010**

Books

- » Ask and It is Given - **Esther Hicks**
- » The Science of Getting Rich – **Wallace Wattles**
- » Wake up and Live - **Dorothea Brande**
- » The Law of Success in 16 lessons – **Napoleon Hill**
- » Think and Grow Rich - **Napoleon Hill**

- » Wishes Fulfilled –**Dr. Wayne Dyer**

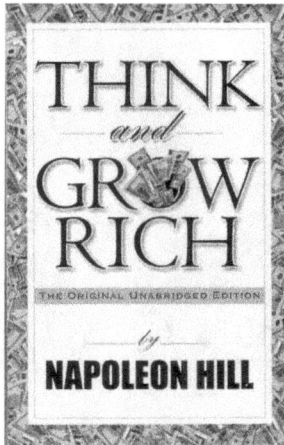

Audios

» Change your Thoughts, Change your Circumstances-**You Are Creators 2**
» How to Train the Mind-**You Are Creators**
» If You Learn This Your Life Will Never Be The Same-**Law of Attraction**
» How to get What You Really Really Really Want- **Deepak Chopra & Dr. Wayne Dyer**

Chapter Fourteen

Definitions
How to's
Affirmations

Definitions

Mediation - A precise technique for resting the mind and attaining a state of consciousness that is totally different from the normal waking state. It is the means for fathoming all the levels of ourselves and finally experiencing the center of consciousness within. Meditation is not a part of any religion; it is a science, which means that the process of meditation follows an order, has definite principles, and produces results that can be verified.

The Law of Attraction - The belief that by focusing on positive or negative thoughts a person brings positive or negative experiences into their life. The teaching is based upon the idea that people and their thoughts are made from "pure energy" and that through the process of "like energy attracting like energy" a person can improve their own health, wealth and personal relationships.

Visualization - A technique involving focusing on positive mental images in order to achieve a goal.

Affirmations - Fostering a belief that a positive statement or words repeated to one's self and written down frequently will achieve success in anything.

Tips on how to:

Meditate

- » Find a quiet place where you will not be disturbed
- » Get into a comfortable position; whether it's sitting or lying down
- » Use a timer if needed; start out with just 5 minutes a day until completely mastered
- » Start with guided meditations found online (optional)
- » Close your eyes and breathe normally, if needed for relaxation; take 5 deep breaths to begin
- » Focus on your eyelids. Thoughts will come but just return your thoughts to the darkness
- » Listen to relaxing and soothing sounds (optional)
- » Do this 3 to 4 time a week, or as often as you like
- » Enjoy

Visualize

- » Relax, turn off all distractions
- » Get an image or images of what you want; be specific. There's a reason for definiteness
- » Concentrate on the images; put yourself in the image already having, being or doing what it is you want
- » See it through your eyes, as if you're physically there, not as if you're looking at yourself through the image
- » Develop a feeling of having or doing what it is you desire. Feel how you will feel once this is a reality. Feelings are very important
- » Maintain these images and feelings for at least 15 minutes per day
- » Open your eyes and declare out loud you will have what you want

Affirmations

Most affirmations start with the two words **I Am** which are very powerful. Confirm what it is you desire using the phrase "**I Am** and whatever it is you want to confirm. Be very mindful when using these two words, stay away from phrases such as; I am Poor or I am Sick, etc. There are also several other affirmations which can be used as well. Here are some of my favorites;

- » I am Healthy
- » I am Wealthy
- » I am Beautiful
- » I am Successful
- » I deserve Abundance in all areas of my Life
- » Prosperity is all around me
- » Joy and Happiness are a constant in my life
- » I Love my Life and the people in my Life

"The Universe is asking…show me your new vibration, I will show you miracles"

I wish everyone Happiness, Health and Wealth!
Blessings!

www.ingramcontent.com/pod-product-compliance
Lightning Source LLC
LaVergne TN
LVHW021352080426
835508LV00020B/2240